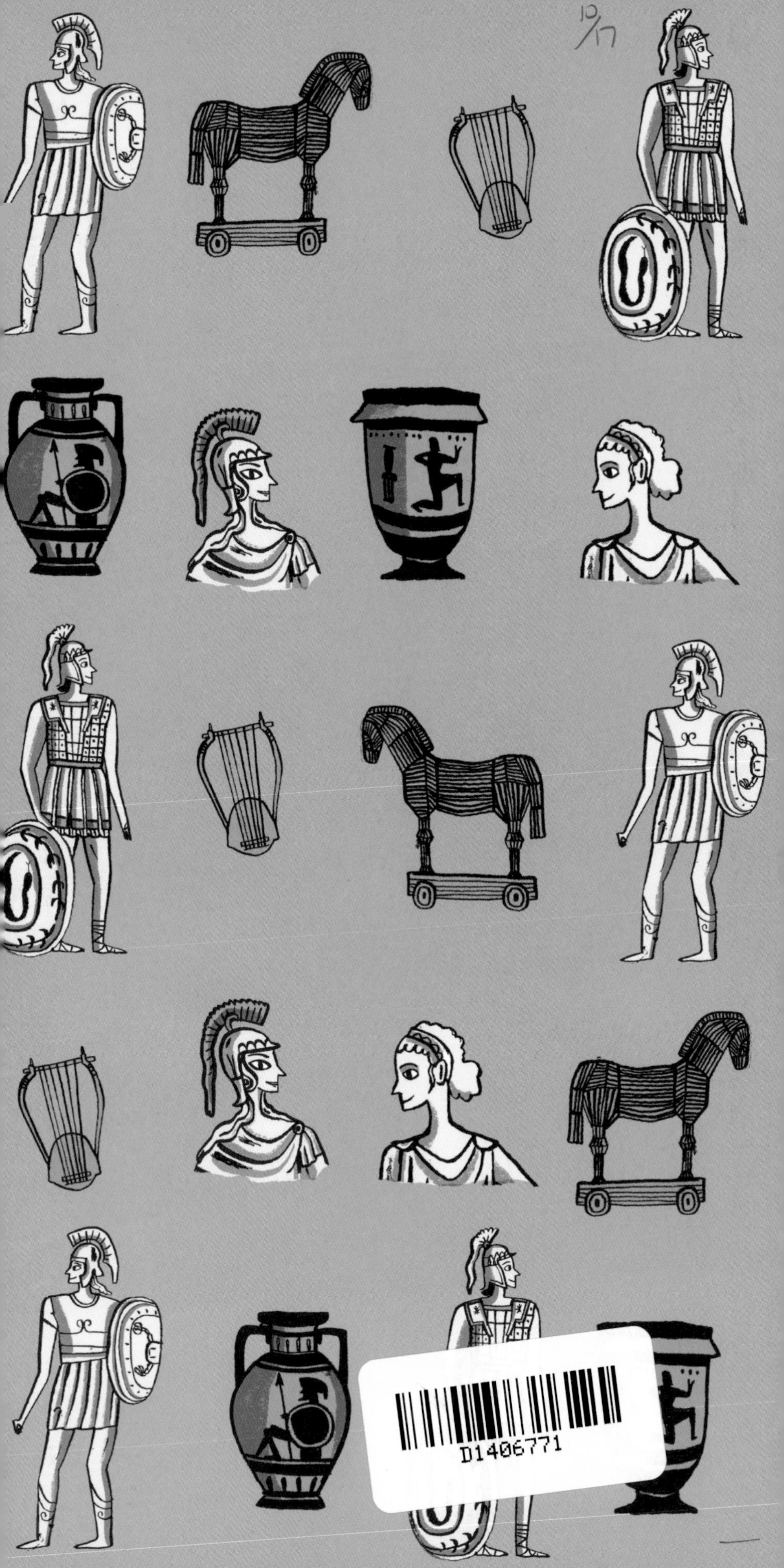

DISCOVER...

THE ANCIENT GREEKS

Illustrated by
Isabel Greenberg

Written by
Imogen Greenberg

Frances Lincoln
Children's Books

Welcome to Ancient Greece

For hundreds of years, the ancient Greeks competed in the Olympic Games, went to war in heroic battles, and recited epic poetry. But who were the ancient Greeks really?

Ancient Greece wasn't a single empire, but hundreds of independent regions called city-states. Each had its own laws and its own culture. But they also shared an idea, across hundreds of miles, that together they were "Greek." They shared a history, they shared ancient stories, and they shared gods. They traded across the Aegean Sea and went to war in the vast Peloponnesian peninsula.

The Greeks are remembered as the founders of democracy, which is a way of ruling where a collection of people, or citizens, vote fairly to decide who represents them and how they should act.

Today, we know a lot about how they lived, thanks to historians and archaeologists. Historians read books and documents that the ancient Greeks left behind. Archaeologists dig up the ruins left behind by the ancient Greeks—from vast temples to the smallest houses—so we know about how they lived.

In this book, you will discover all kinds of secrets about the ancient Greeks...and if you're wondering where and when these things happened, turn to the back, where you'll find a fold-out map and timeline. Now, come and meet your guide!

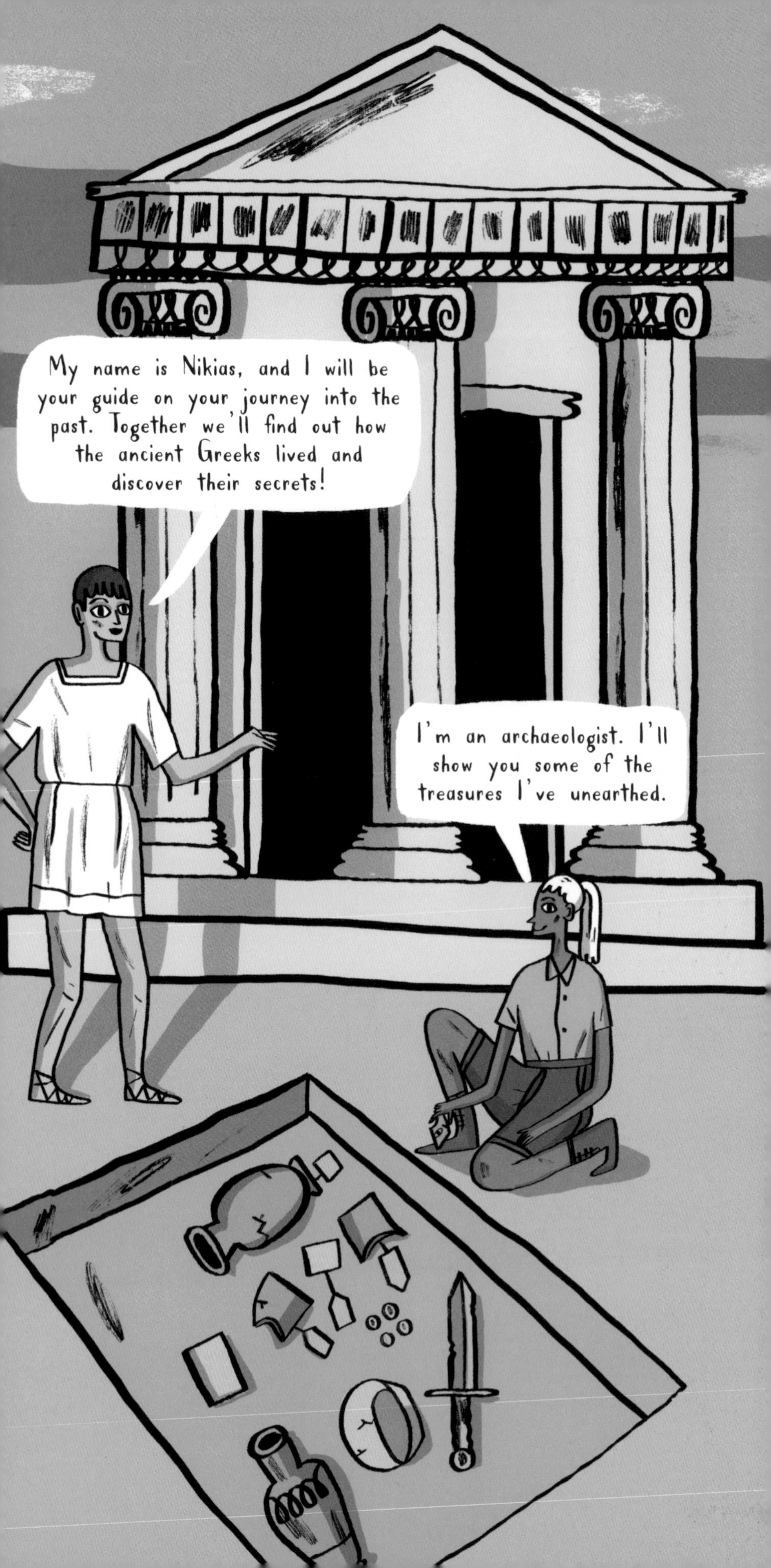
My name is Nikias, and I will be your guide on your journey into the past. Together we'll find out how the ancient Greeks lived and discover their secrets!
I'm an archaeologist. I'll show you some of the treasures I've unearthed.

GREEK CITIES

Ancient Greece was made up of hundreds of independent regions, called city-states. Each had its own citizens, its own laws, and its own way of doing things.

Here in Athens, we founded democracy and everyone else copied us.

In Corinth we're famous for pottery, which will last way longer than this "democracy" thing...

But across the whole of ancient Greece, they had a shared idea that they were all "Greek" and that their neighbors were nowhere near as good as them.

They traded across the vast seas of the Aegean, they went to war when tensions arose between the cities, and they competed in the heroic Olympic Games.

Take that, Spartan!

Whatever. I'm going to beat you in the Marathon this summer!

Athens and Sparta were two very powerful cities that often went to war against each other. It all came to a head when they formed vast alliances with other city-states across Greece, gathering support against each other.

GREEK RULE

There were three types of rule in ancient Greece: tyranny, oligarchy, and democracy.

TYRANNY

A tyrant was one person who ruled the city-state by unjustly overturning the current rulers. They were often very popular when they first came to power, because they promised the people lots of great new things to rationalize removing the old government.

OLIGARCHY

An oligarchy was when a small group of people ruled all of society. They were usually wealthy and inherited their importance in society through their family.

DEMOCRACY

Democracy began in Athens. The word comes from the Greek word, *demoKratia*: "rule of the people." A large group of people ruled together by voting for representatives and voting on the best action to taKe.

A man named Cleisthenes invented democracy in 507 BC. Cleisthenes ruled by himself after he overthrew somebody else, but he then decided to share power among the citizens of Athens. He created a large council of people who made decisions and promised to do what was best for the people.

GREEK SOCIETY

In Athens, all citizens were equal in the democracy. This meant that they could vote and they could stand to represent the people in the council. But not everyone was a citizen.

To be a citizen you had to be an adult man who had completed military training.

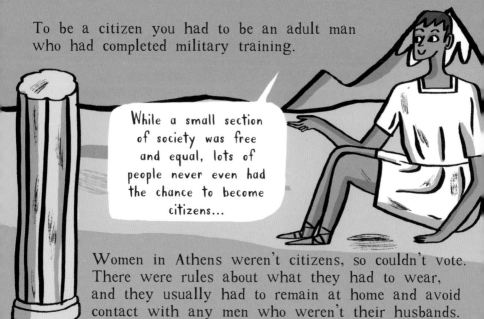

While a small section of society was free and equal, lots of people never even had the chance to become citizens...

Women in Athens weren't citizens, so couldn't vote. There were rules about what they had to wear, and they usually had to remain at home and avoid contact with any men who weren't their husbands.

Don't forget us women!

VOTES FOR WOMEN

Or us slaves, either.

There were thousands of slaves in Athens who worked on the land or in mines and fought in the army. They were the possessions of Athenian citizens, along with their families, and didn't get paid for any of the work they did.

Ancient Greek men usually dressed in a tunic. They came in all different sizes, shapes, lengths, and colors. Women wore something similar, but theirs usually went down to their ankles. Ordinary clothes were made of wool, but some people had ones made of more expensive linen or silk.

Madam, where did you get that tunic? Does it come in pink?

Ancient Greek houses had rooms for entertaining or having dinner parties. But these were only for the men. There were separate entrances to the houses so that guests wouldn't accidentally bump into women. Ancient Greek boys went to school, but girls weren't allowed.

That's sort of unfair, right?

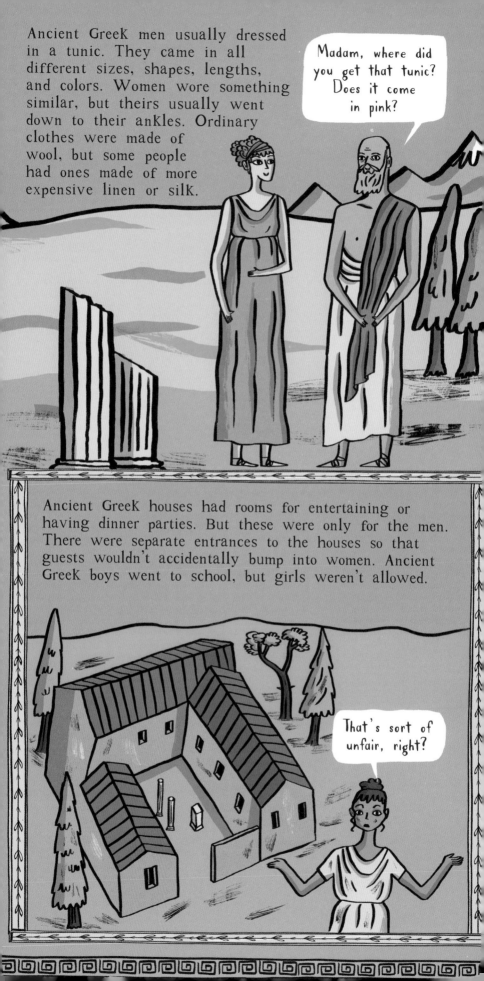

HALL OF

C. 540 BC-480 BC
LEONIDAS was the warrior-King of Sparta. He led the Spartans in the Persian Wars, trying to stop the Persians from invading the rest of Greece. He died in battle.

LEONIDAS

C. 495 BC-429 BC
PERICLES was a statesman, general, and famous orator (a great speech-maker). He led the Athenians in the Peloponnesian Wars.

PERICLES

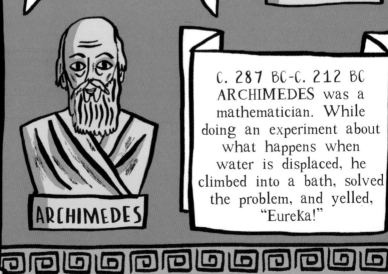

C. 287 BC-C. 212 BC
ARCHIMEDES was a mathematician. While doing an experiment about what happens when water is displaced, he climbed into a bath, solved the problem, and yelled, "Eureka!"

ARCHIMEDES

FAME

SAPPHO

?-C. 570 BC
SAPPHO was a poet from Lesbos. She wrote beautiful poetry that tells us about the lives of women in ancient Greece.

HERODOTUS

C. 484 BC-C. 425 BC
HERODOTUS was known as the Father of History. He wrote the first history book, telling of the Persian Wars and how the Greeks came to beat the Persians in 480 BC.

AESOP

C. 620 BC-564 BC
AESOP was a writer who wrote short stories called fables, which have morals or lessons in them. You've probably heard of some of them, like "The Tortoise and the Hare."

PERSIAN WARS

In the 5th century BC, when ancient Greece wasn't very powerful and the city-states were weak and divided, they faced a great and powerful enemy.

The Persian Empire stretched for thousands of miles and had a large army. As the empire got more and more powerful, they set their sights on the Greek city-states. In 490 BC, under their ruler Darius, they marched on mainland Greece.

> Those Greeks think they're so great? See how they do against my mighty army!

But at the last minute, the Athenians won a triumphant victory at the Battle of Marathon, and the Persian army escaped back to Asia.

Darius's son Xerxes vowed to try again. In 480 BC, he crossed the Hellespont (the stretch of sea between Europe and Asia), with wooden boats strung together to make a bridge. He had an army of thousands of soldiers, cavalry, and even elephants.

> Bridge is looking solid, Your Majesty!

> Good work, foot soldier! We'll show those Greeks this time!

The Persians marched through Greece, and the people fled. When the army reached Athens, they burnt down the Acropolis—the center of the city. The Greek states were in uproar. They decided to consult the oracle at Delphi...

The Greek states were baffled. How could a wooden wall save them from the Persians? Then they suddenly decided that the oracle meant a wooden wall of ships!

The allied Greek states defeated the Persians in a great sea battle, called the Battle of Salamis. Then the Greeks came together one last time to defeat the Persians in an enormous land battle, called the Battle of Plataea.

ALEXANDER THE GREAT

Alexander the Great was the King of Macedonia, from 336 BC to 323 BC. The Macedonians had always been the less powerful neighbors of the Greeks. When the 20-year-old Macedonian King Alexander set out on a great expedition to conquer the Persian Empire, everyone underestimated him.

Alexander conquered the great cities of the Persian Empire, including Babylon, Susa, and Persepolis. When the Persian emperor Darius was murdered by his own men, Alexander declared himself Emperor of Persia. He had conquered more than any Greek or Macedonian before him.

He marched his army toward India, where he faced the great King Porus and his army of elephants in an epic battle. Alexander rode into battle on his trusty steed Bucephalus.

Alexander defeated Porus in the Battle of the Hydaspes River, but his beloved horse Bucephalus died. His men refused to fight anymore, so they marched to Babylon, where Alexander fell ill and died. Within hours, his commanders were squabbling over who would rule his vast empire.

GREEK RELIGION

The Greeks built temples for gods as a "home" for them. The Athenians named their city after Athena and built a temple for her in the most important site, the Acropolis.

In temples, people left offerings for the gods, to ask for their help with things like a good harvest, lots of children, or a safe journey.

The more impressive the temple, the more thankful the god.

The Greeks celebrated special festivals to the gods and goddesses. The whole city would gather, and they would parade through the streets, offering sacrifices and prayers. There would be singing and dancing, and an enormous feast.

Any excuse for a party, eh?

When the ancient Greeks had a really difficult decision to make, they often consulted an oracle. Oracles were messengers for the gods and were supposed to help ordinary people with everyday problems.

There was one particular oracle that was famous all across Greece and beyond. Cities used to consult the oracle of Delphi on very important issues, like what laws to pass and whether or not to go to war.

The Greeks had many gods and goddesses, who lived on top of Mount Olympus. They were like a big family, who loved each other but also fought all the time. Zeus was the King of the gods and ruled the earth and sky, hurling thunder down from the mountaintops. His brother Hades ruled the Underworld—the world of the dead—while his brother Poseidon ruled the seas.

Zeus's wife, Hera, was the queen of the gods and the protector of women. When Hera and Zeus fought, the earth shook and chaos broke out. Aphrodite was the goddess of love. Hermes was the messenger god, and he had amazing winged sandals!

The ancient Greeks were fascinated by their own history. The greatest story of all was the *Trojan War*, which took place hundreds of years before. Everyone knew the stories, because the poet Homer composed epic poems about it.

> Helen, I love you! Run away with me?

> I'm already married to King Menelaus... but okay!

THE ILIAD

The Iliad told the story of Paris of Troy and Helen—King Menelaus's wife—who ran away together. For revenge, Menelaus and his brother Agamemnon united all of Greece to go to war against Troy.

When Paris ran away, his brother Hector, Prince of Troy, fought Menelaus for years to protect Troy from the Greeks. But also fighting for Menelaus was the warrior Achilles.

> I'm Hector, Prince of Troy, and these Greeks won't get off my beach. And Paris won't even get out here himself.

> I'm Achilles, and I will vanquish all men who stand between me and eternal glory!

As a child, Achilles's mother dipped him in the River Styx to make him invincible, but the spot where she held his ankles didn't touch the water. This was his only weak spot! Achilles killed Hector in single combat, so Paris shot an arrow straight through Achilles's heel—killing him, too.

After ten years of war, the Greeks had an idea. They built a giant wooden horse, hid inside it, and left it in front of the enormous walls of Troy. The Trojans thought the horse was a gift from the gods, so they wheeled it inside their city.

When the Trojans were sleeping, the Greeks jumped out of the horse and burned Troy to the ground, defeating the Trojans at last.

THE ODYSSEY

Homer's second poem, *The Odyssey*, tells of how the heroic warrior Odysseus got lost on his journey home from Troy.

Odysseus and his sailors faced great enemies, like the one-eyed monster Cyclops and the Sirens, who lured sailors to their island. But Odysseus got home just in time to stop his wife, Penelope, from being married off to someone else!

JASON AND THE ARGONAUTS

The Greeks had lots of other great myths, or stories, too. *Jason and the Argonauts* told of the dashing Prince of Iolkos, Jason, whose uncle Pelias stole his throne. Pelias told Jason that he would give his kingdom back, on one condition...

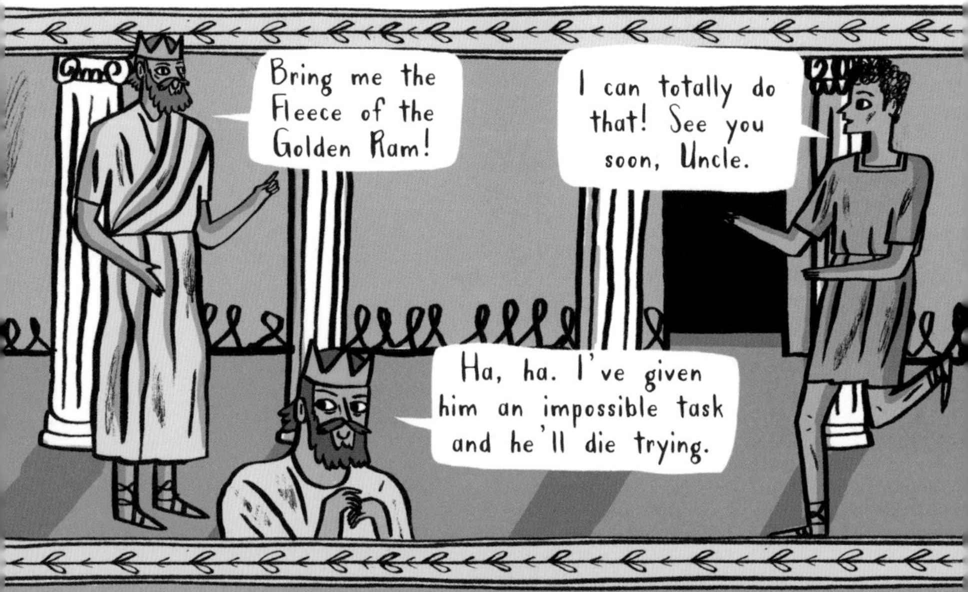
Bring me the Fleece of the Golden Ram!
I can totally do that! See you soon, Uncle.
Ha, ha. I've given him an impossible task and he'll die trying.

Jason set out with 50 sailors on a ship called the *Argo*. Together, they were the Argonauts. Along the way, they found a cursed colony of women who murdered their husbands, and rescued a blind prophet, Phineus, from a bunch of Harpies. Then they reached the land of Colchis.

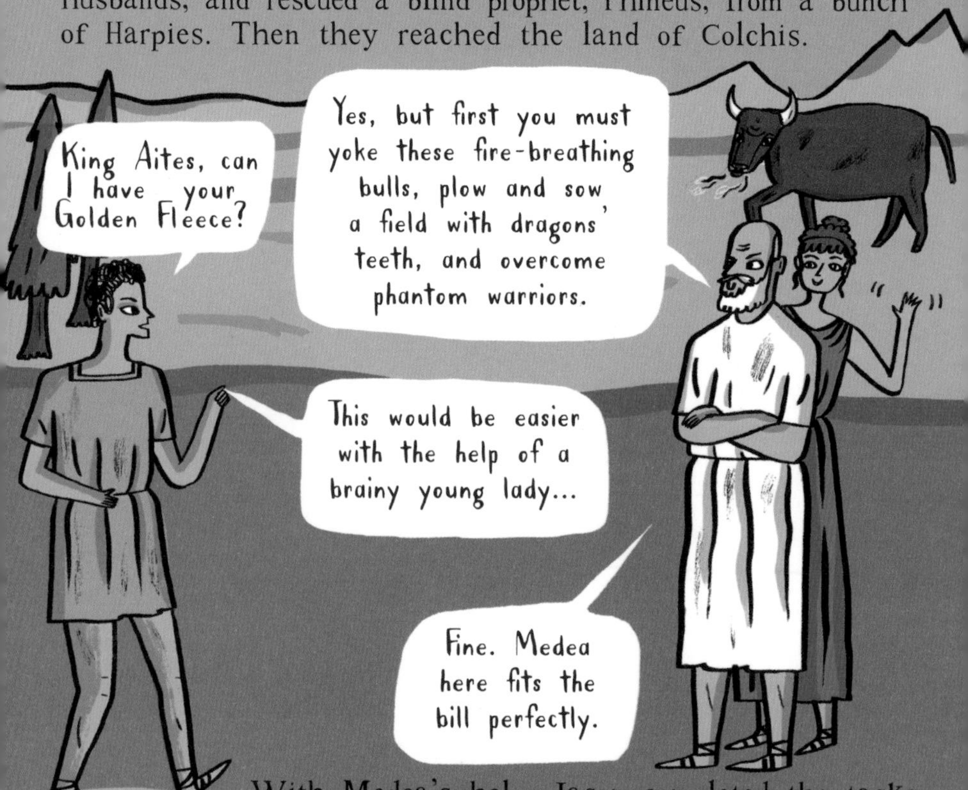
King Aites, can I have your Golden Fleece?
Yes, but first you must yoke these fire-breathing bulls, plow and sow a field with dragons' teeth, and overcome phantom warriors.
This would be easier with the help of a brainy young lady...
Fine. Medea here fits the bill perfectly.

With Medea's help, Jason completed the tasks and was granted the Golden Fleece. He returned home to take his throne, with Medea at his side.

THESEUS AND THE MINOTAUR

Theseus, the young son of King Aegeus of Athens, was brave (and maybe a little stupid). Every year, seven people from Athens were sacrificed to the mighty Minotaur—a beast that was half man and half bull—living in a labyrinth on the island of Crete. Theseus volunteered and when he arrived, he met Princess Ariadne, daughter of King Minos of Crete.

She gave him a ball of thread and told him to unravel it as he navigated the labyrinth, to find his way out again. Theseus battled the mighty Minotaur in the labyrinth and Killed it. With Ariadne's trick, he found his way out.

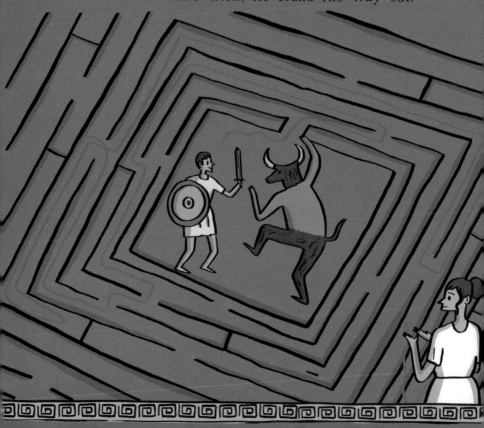

Ancient Athens was famous for its theater. The Athenians built an enormous open-air theater next to the Acropolis, called the Theater of Dionysus. Theater became so popular that it spread across all of Greece. Plays were divided into two Kinds:

Comedies...

...and tragedies.

Tragedies were sad and dramatic, and often had lessons or morals in them. The most famous writers of tragedy were Sophocles, Aeschylus, and Euripides.

Guys, I've got a great idea: *The Oresteia.* Orestes sets out to avenge his father's murder —

In mine, a king named Oedipus kills his father and marries his mother!

SOPHOCLES

AESCHYLU

URIPIDES

Well, mine's about Medea, who kills her ex-husband's wife and children. I'll definitely win at the Dionysia festival!

Ugh, Euripides, your acceptance speeches go on forever.

Comedies were hilarious, and always had a happy ending. Aristophanes was your guy when it came to comedy!

That's right, ladies. These useless men have been fighting for years, and I'm just not having it anymore.

Lysistrata is all about one woman who tried to end the Peloponnesian Wars. She persuaded all the women in Greece to refuse to speak to their husbands until they negotiated peace.

The Knights was a play that was very rude about Cleon, a powerful Athenian general. Because Aristophanes's plays were very funny but also about real events, they could influence public opinion about very powerful people.

I don't think Aristophanes was invited over for dinner very much.

PHILOSOPHY

The ancient Athenians were also famous for their schools of philosophy. Boys were trained in academies, learning about history, science, mathematics, and philosophy. The most famous Athenian philosophers were Socrates, Plato, and Aristotle.

Socrates thought about what was right and wrong, and taught his students to think.

I cannot teach anybody anything. I can only make them think. To find yourself, think for yourself.

SOCRATES

Socrates was smart and humble, and his students loved him. But soon the most powerful men in Athens were jealous and put him on trial for corrupting the youth of Athens. They sentenced him to death by drinking hemlock, a powerful poison.

It's okay, guys. I'll take one for the team.

He even makes us look bad when he's dying...

Plato was a student of Socrates, and he became a famous philosopher himself. His most famous idea is called *The Cave* and is an allegory for what life was like when you didn't study philosophy.

DEEP, MAN!

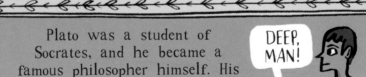

PLATO

A philosopher is like a prisoner freed from the cave, who knows that shadows aren't real, but just shadows.

In Plato's theory, those who don't study philosophy are like a group of people chained in a cave, facing a wall. They can't see anything happening behind them—they can only see the shadows of what's happening on the wall in front of them.

Aristotle was a pupil of Plato's. He wrote about lots of things, like ethics, politics, logic, poetry, theater, and music. He was so famous across Greece that he became a tutor to Alexander the Great when he was a young boy.

THE OLYMPIC GAMES

The most important festivals in ancient Greece were the Games, where cities came together to compete against each other. The most famous of all were the Olympic Games, held at the foot of Mount Olympus. The great Greek hero Hercules named them the Olympic Games.

At the Games, (often naked) athletes competed in lots of different challenges. There was the pentathlon, which included five events: jumping, discus, javelin throws, a race, and wrestling. There was also boxing, wrestling, and chariot racing.

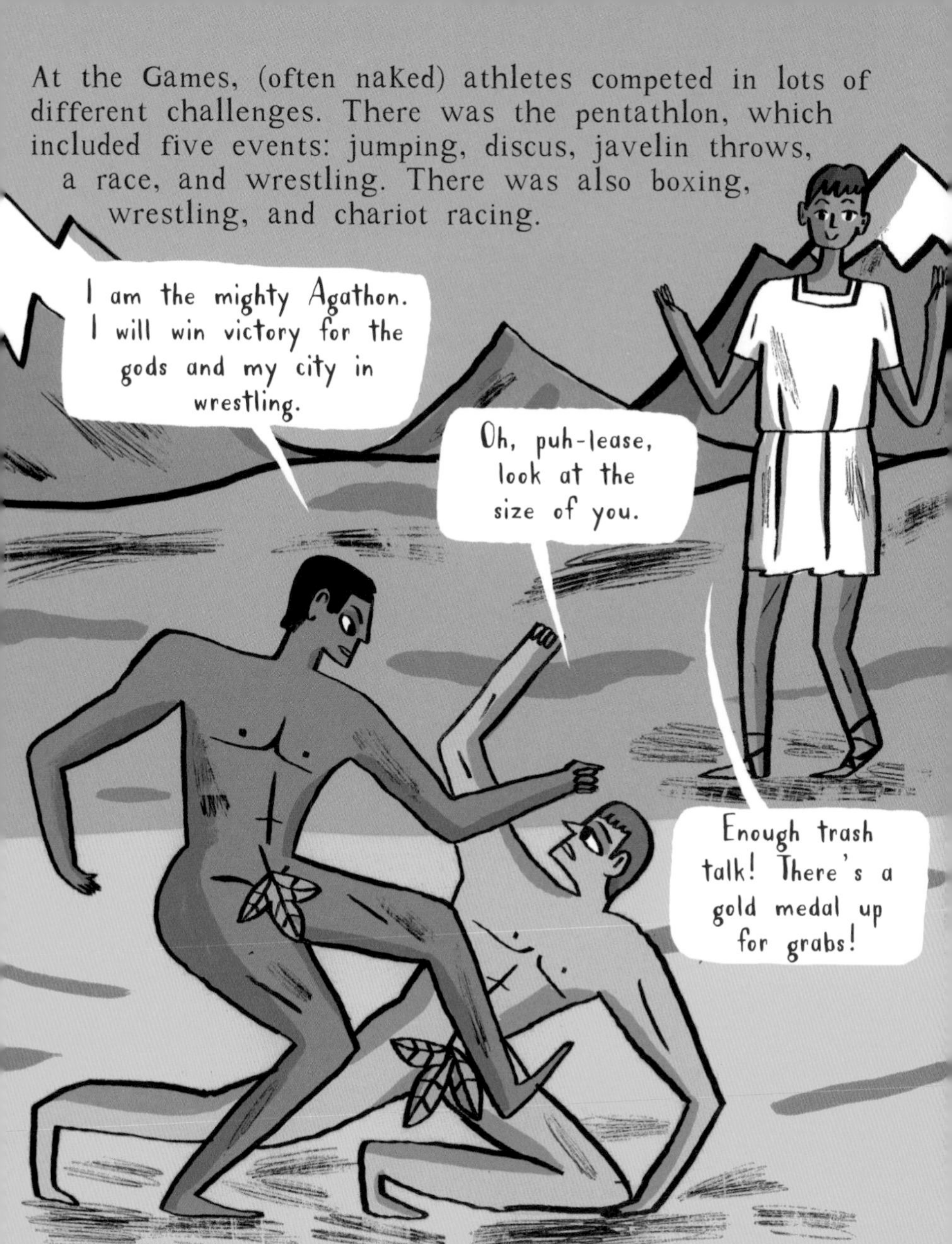
I am the mighty Agathon. I will win victory for the gods and my city in wrestling.
Oh, puh-lease, look at the size of you.
Enough trash talk! There's a gold medal up for grabs!

The winner of each event was given an olive branch or olive wreath, which was worn like a crown. They also won prize money, and sometimes vats of olive oil or other precious goods.

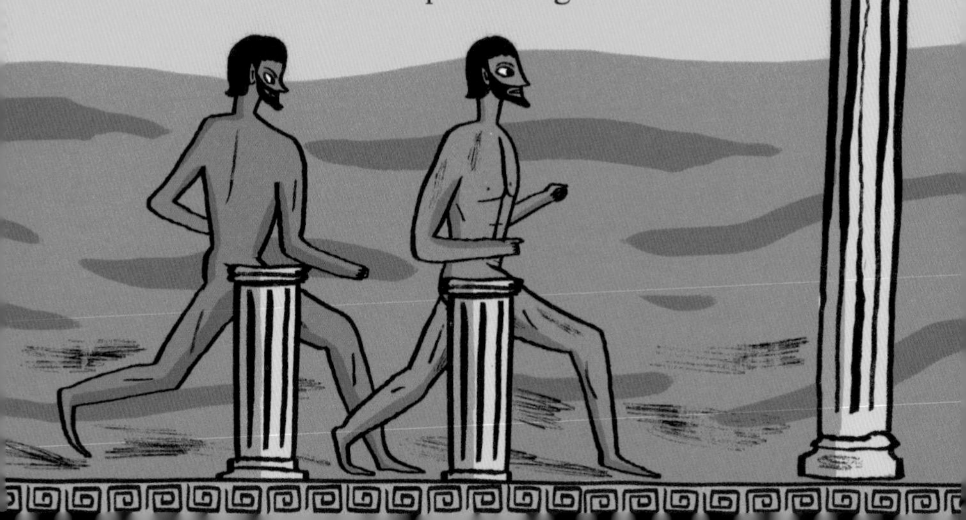

Archaeologists dig up amazing Greek things every day. Each time we find something, it tells us more about how the ancient Greeks lived. This is a typical Greek city:

It had an agora. That means "gathering place" and was a central, public square in the city.

There was a theater, where the great plays would have been performed.

It would have had fancy houses made of stone and decorated with mosaics. Most houses were made of mud bricks, so they crumbled away, but stone lasts thousands of years— which is how archaeologists know lots about the big, fancy buildings the Greeks built!

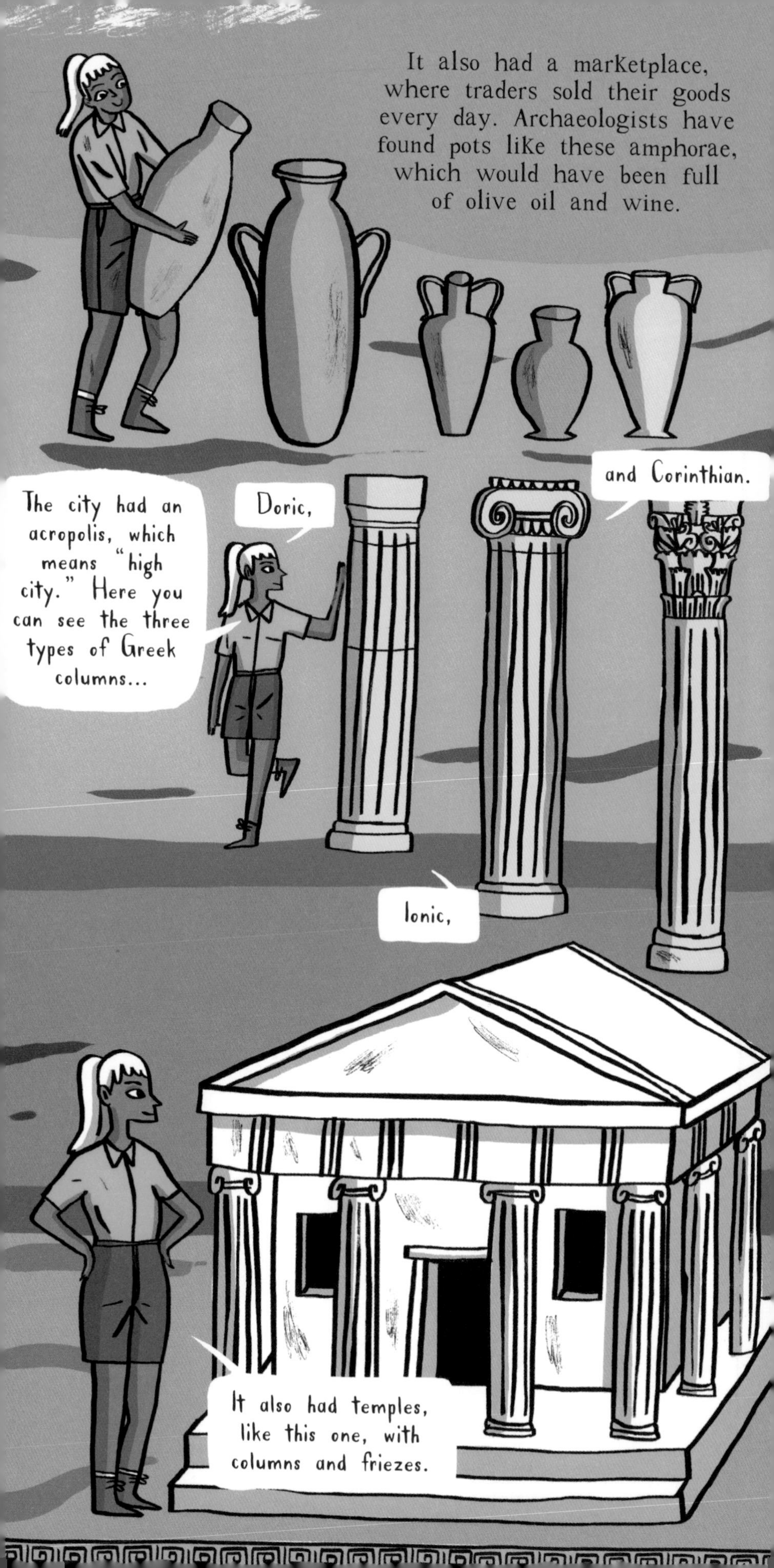
It also had a marketplace, where traders sold their goods every day. Archaeologists have found pots like these amphorae, which would have been full of olive oil and wine.
The city had an acropolis, which means "high city." Here you can see the three types of Greek columns...
Doric,
Ionic,
and Corinthian.
It also had temples, like this one, with columns and friezes.

Isabel Greenberg is a London-based comic artist, illustrator, and writer. She enjoys illustrating all things historical.

Imogen Greenberg is a London-based writer, who loves to write about history.

Quarto is the authority on a wide range of topics.
Quarto educates, entertains and enriches the lives of our readers—enthusiasts and lovers of hands-on living.
www.quartoknows.com

First published in the USA in 2017 by
Frances Lincoln Children's Books, an imprint of Quarto Inc.,
142 W 36th St, 4th Floor, New York, NY 10018, USA
QuartoKnows.com
Visit our blogs at QuartoKnows.com

ISBN 978-1-84780-951-3
Illustrated digitally

Set in Tom's New Roman and Campland

Printed in China

9 8 7 6 5 4 3 2 1

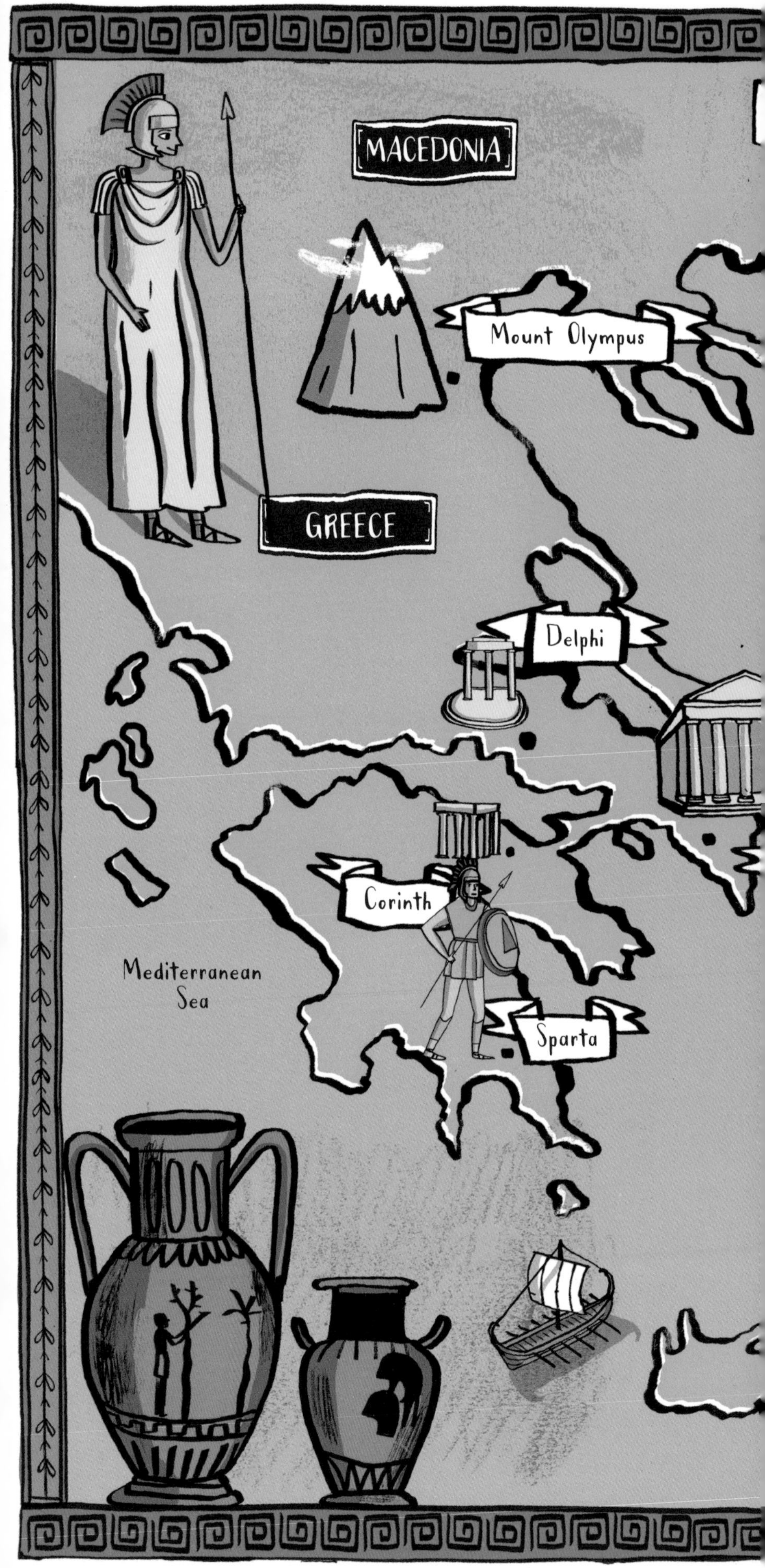
MACEDONIA
Mount Olympus
GREECE
Delphi
Corinth
Mediterranean Sea
Sparta

TIMELINE OF THE ANCIENT GREEKS

The ancient Greeks lived and ruled in the Mediterranean for hundreds of years.
Here are some of the most important events that happened in ancient Greece.

Way back when
Hercules invents the
Olympic Games.

Way back when...
Jason returns home
with the Golden Fleece.

Way back when...
The Trojans are
defeated and the city
of Troy is sacked.

Way back when...
Theseus defeats the Minotaur.

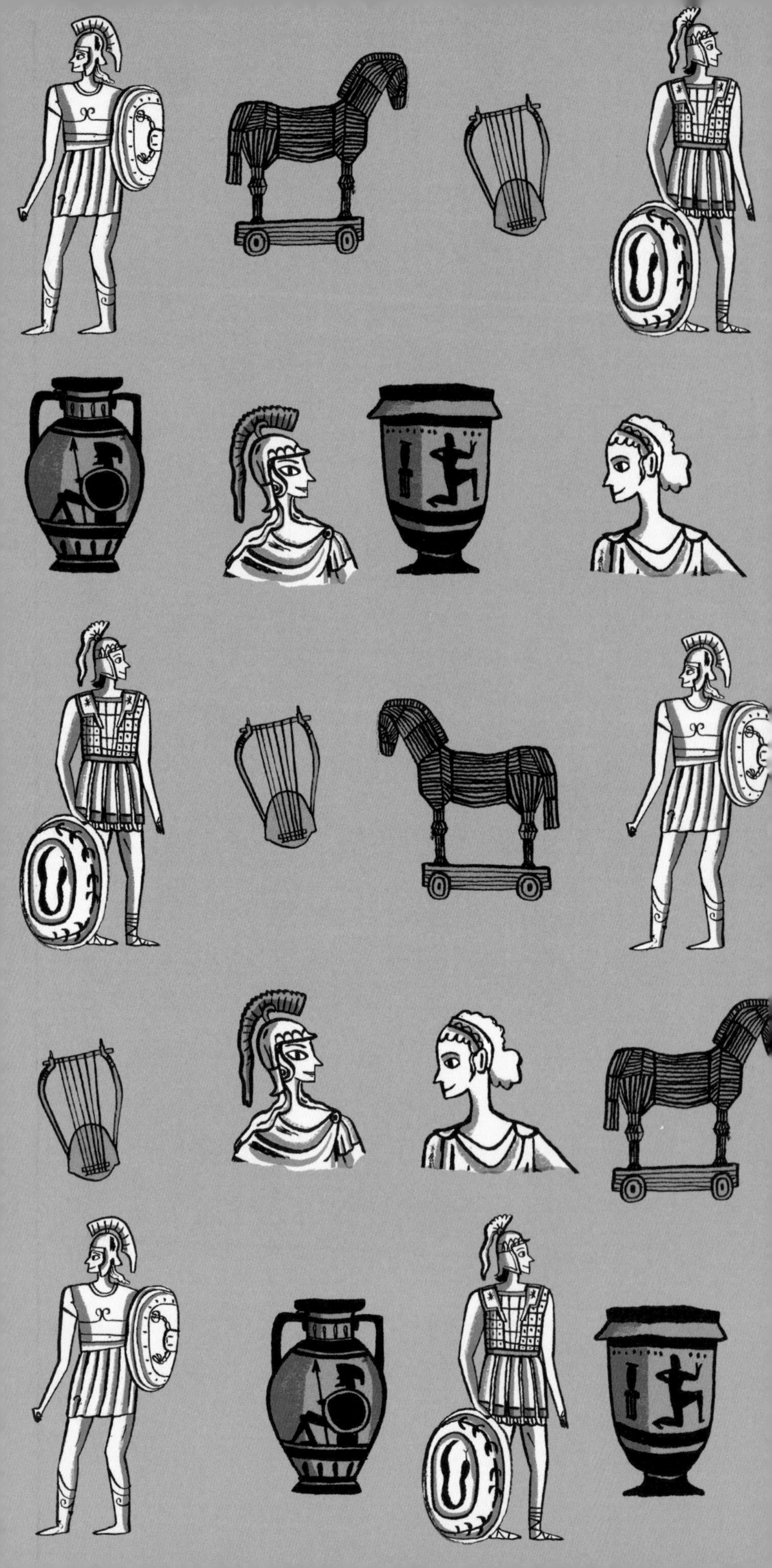